Mental Math
Kids Can't Resist!

Tips, Shortcut Strategies, and
60 Fun Practice Pages That Reinforce
Essential Math Skills and
Boost Test Scores

by Richard Piccirilli

This work is dedicated to my wife, Fraye, who makes living an exciting adventure.

Acknowledgments

I easily recognize the value of being surrounded by supportive people. To my family, who makes it all worthwhile, I love you. To my parents, Domenico and Frances, who have left an indelible mark on me, thank you for teaching me the meaning of hard work. To my many elementary students with whom I have worked over the last 33 years, thank you for your inspiration, for teaching me how to teach math, and for always bringing out the best in me as a teacher. To Linda Decker, thank you for typing the manuscript.

– RSJP

Cover design by **James Sarfati**

Interior design by **Holly Grundon**

Cover illustration by **Rick Stromoski**

Interior illustrations by **Mike Moran**

Copyright © 2000 by **Richard Piccirilli**

Contents

Introduction

This book gives teachers practical and easy-to-use ideas for teaching mental-math skills to students in grades 2–4. The activities are designed to teach and reinforce mental-math skills, as well as give students opportunities to use their newly acquired skill.

You'll find the activities easy to integrate into your curriculum either as lessons in mental math or as a supplement to other daily math activity. Most valuable perhaps are the many activities that relate mental-math strategies to learning the basic number facts.

This book helps students become flexible thinkers with numbers and encourages them to be inventive when encountering new number situations. The activities expose students to new opportunities for using mental-math skills in daily situations in and out of school.

With mental math, students develop a positive attitude toward numbers. They visualize numbers, retain them in their heads, and develop a sense of the quantities numbers represent. They also develop other skills important to overall math achievement—place value, spatial ability, number facts, computation, problem solving, estimation, number properties, and writing about math. As a result, mental math boosts students' confidence. In a very short time they can come to feel smart!

What is mental math?

Mental math is finding answers to number problems or situations using only your head. It is a creative process, which requires you to invent unique mental procedures to deal with numbers in very simple ways. Mental math does not use pencil and paper, calculators, or other recording devices. Instead, it employs strategies that help you to see relationships among numbers and compute them mentally.

There are two facets to mental math: First, we use mental math to find estimated answers. Then, we use mental math to find exact answers. This second facet is often referred to as **mental computation**, which is the focus of this book.

Why is it important to teach young children mental math?

It is important to teach young children mental math because it is a valuable, useful skill and a powerful tool.

The National Council of Teachers of Mathematics (NCTM) has awakened the need to teach mental math. The newly released NCTM Standards 2000 states:

> Students should select appropriate methods and tools for computing with whole numbers from among mental computation, estimation, calculators, and paper and pencil according to the context and nature of the computation, and use the selected method or tool.

What are some noteworthy features of this book?

The activities in this book are appropriate for grades 2–4, as well as for students of varying abilities. Basic exercises help young students build a foundation in math, while more difficult exercises challenge students who are more skillful in math. Clear and simple directions as well as model examples help students understand their tasks very quickly.

Activities cover topics in the primary math curriculum: number sense, number facts, addition and subtraction, with attention to the early concepts of multiplication and division.

You can easily make transparencies from any activity page. Pages that feature this transparency logo at right can be used as a focal point for whole- or small-group lessons using the overhead projector.

"Write About It" questions throughout the book ask students to reflect, integrate, apply, and consolidate what they have learned in mental math.

What is the best way to use this book?

The following suggestions should serve as a guide to help you make the best use of the book, with the least amount of time and effort.

1. Become familiar with the topic you will be teaching. This will help you prepare lessons that are meaningful and fun.

2. Before assigning student activity pages, discuss the topic from the assigned page. Encourage students to share their thoughts and ideas on how to solve practice examples before teaching the strategies. This is where important learning will occur.

3. Encourage students to share their strategies with you, their classmates, and their family.

4. Take advantage of the Skill Builders activities. They introduce children to the usefulness and application of mental math and build confidence early in their math careers.

5. As opportunities arise, refer to ideas previously learned. When assigning practice activities from textbooks, have students look for examples that can be done mentally, or have them estimate some of their answers before completing the assigned examples.

6. Use the activities in this book as models to make your own mental-math worksheets.

The Basic Mental-Math Strategies

The three mental-math strategies for grades 2–4 are:

- ● **MAKE EASY NUMBERS**
- ● **BREAK UP NUMBERS**
- ● **COMPENSATE**

Mental computation may use one strategy or a combination of these three strategies. For example, in making easy numbers, you may have to break up numbers. Or, to make easy numbers you may have to compensate.

Students should be aware of these strategies and be able to identify which ones they're using. Below are examples of each strategy:

1 MAKE EASY NUMBERS

Easy numbers are numbers that are easy to compute without using a calculator or pencil and paper. Examples of easy numbers are numbers that end in 0, like 10, 20, 30, 40, 50. Here are some examples of numbers that are easy to add, subtract, multiply, and divide:

10 + 20
Add 1 + 2 = 3
Put 0 next to the 3
10 + 20 = 30

50 – 30
Subtract 5 – 3 = 2
Put 0 next to the 2
50 – 30 = 20

96 x 10
Multiply 96 x 1 = 96
Put 0 next to the 96
96 x 10 = 960

360 ÷ 9
Divide 36 ÷ 9 = 4
Put 0 next to the 4
360 ÷ 9 = 40

You can regroup numbers to make easy numbers:

3 + 76 + 7
= (3 + 7) + 76
= 10 + 76
= 86

5 x 47 x 2
= (5 x 2) x 47
= 10 x 47
= 470

87 – 12
= 87 – 10 – 2
= 77 – 2
= 75

2 BREAKING UP NUMBERS

Breaking up numbers means separating numbers to make them easier to compute. Here are some examples:

38 + 46
= (30 + 8) + (40 + 6)
= (30 + 40) + (8 + 6)
= 70 + 14
= 70 + 10 + 4
= 80 + 4
= 84

4 x 18
= 4 x (10 + 8)
= (4 x 10) + (4 x 8)
= 40 + 32
= 40 + 30 + 2
= 70 + 2
= 72

93 – 16
= 93 – 10 – 6
= 83 – 6
= 77

48 ÷ 4
= (40 + 8) ÷ 4
= (40 ÷ 4) + (8 ÷ 4)
= 10 + 2
= 12

3 COMPENSATION

To compensate, you can do one of the following:
- Adjust one of the numbers and then adjust the answer.
- Adjust both numbers. Then it's not necessary to adjust the answer.

Here are examples when one of the numbers and the answer are adjusted:

46 + 19
Add 1 to 19 to make 20:
    19 + 1 = 20
Then add 46 and 20: 46 + 20 = 66
Subtract 1 from 66 to
    compensate: 66 – 1 = 65
So 46 + 19 = 65

137 – 98
Add 2 to 98 to make 100:
    98 + 2 = 100
Then subtract 137 and 100: 137 – 100 = 37
Add 2 to 37 to compensate: 37 + 2 = 39
So 137 – 98 = 39

Here are examples when both numbers in the equation are adjusted:

46 + 19
Add 1 to 19: 19 + 1 = 20
Compensate by subtracting
    1 from 46: 46 – 1 = 45
Add 45 + 20 = 65
So 46 + 19 = 65

137 – 98
Add 2 to 98: 98 + 2 = 100
Compensate by adding 2 to 137:
    137 + 2 = 139
Subtract 139 – 100 = 39
So 137 – 98 = 39

MENTAL-MATH STRATEGIES: MAKE EASY NUMBERS

Look for Easy Numbers for E-Z Addition

Directions: Solve the problems below by making easy numbers. Look for numbers that add to 10, 20, 30, or other easy tens numbers. See the examples here.

Examples:

20 + 4 = 24	20 + 30 = 50	6 + 8 + 4 = 6 + 4 + 8 = 10 + 8 = 18	5 + 4 + 10 + 6 = 4 + 6 + 5 + 10 = 10 + 5 + 10 = 10 + 10 + 5 = 25

1. 7 + 3 + 5 = _____

2. 5 + 9 + 5 = _____

3. 4 + 4 + 6 = _____

4. 9 + 8 + 1 = _____

5. 2 + 7 + 8 = _____

6. 7 + 18 + 2 = _____

7. 29 + 10 + 1 = _____

8. 17 + 6 + 3 = _____

9. 25 + 8 + 5 = _____

10. 36 + 4 + 7 = _____

11. 52 + 7 + 1 + 8 = _____

12. 75 + 3 + 5 = _____

Write About It

What do you look for when making easy numbers?

_____

_____

MENTAL-MATH STRATEGIES: MAKE EASY NUMBERS

Look for More Easy Numbers in Addition

Directions: Solve the problems below by making easy numbers. Look for numbers that add to 10, 20, 30, or other easy tens numbers. Before you start, look at the examples.

Examples of easy numbers:

60 + 7 = 67	6 + 28 + 4 = 6 + 4 + 28 = 10 + 28 = 38	7 + 16 + 3 + 20 = 10 + 16 + 20 = 26 + 20 = 46

1. 8 + 12 + 2 = _____

2. 8 + 17 + 2 = _____

3. 23 + 14 + 6 = _____

4. 14 + 25 + 6 = _____

5. 32 + 8 + 40 = _____

6. 87 + 6 + 4 = _____

7. 25 + 25 + 12 = _____

8. 95 + 14 + 5 = _____

9. 9 + 110 + 21 = _____

10. 22 + 8 + 160 = _____

11. 37 + 14 + 3 + 6 = _____

12. 5 + 23 + 55 + 10 = _____

13. 6 + 122 + 8 + 4 = _____

14. 340 + 3 + 7 + 12 = _____

15. 13 + 418 + 7 + 4 = _____

Write About It

How did you solve problem 12?

_____

_____

Make Easy Numbers Using 10 and 100

To make easy numbers, first multiply numbers that result in either 10 or 100. Then multiply the rest of the numbers in the equation. For example:

$2 \times 9 \times 5$
$= (2 \times 5) \times 9$
$= 10 \times 9$
$= 90$

Directions: Make easy numbers to solve the problems below. Draw a line to match the problem to the answer.

1.	$2 \times 9 \times 5 =$	a.	300
2.	$10 \times 3 \times 10 =$	b.	800
3.	$5 \times 13 \times 2 =$	c.	250
4.	$2 \times 5 \times 37 =$	d.	600
5.	$50 \times 7 \times 2 =$	e.	700
6.	$4 \times 8 \times 25 =$	f.	90
7.	$50 \times 9 \times 2 =$	g.	500
8.	$5 \times 5 \times 5 \times 2 =$	h.	370
9.	$2 \times 2 \times 5 \times 3 =$	i.	60
10.	$2 \times 10 \times 5 \times 5 =$	j.	900
11.	$1 \times 2 \times 4 \times 2 \times 5 =$	k.	130
12.	$2 \times 3 \times 5 \times 4 \times 5 =$	l.	80

MENTAL-MATH STRATEGIES: BREAKING UP NUMBERS

Using Patterns of 10

23 + 30?
Hmm... 23, 33, 43, 53!

Directions: To solve the problems below, break up the numbers into groups of 10. See the examples here.

Examples:

23 + 30 Break up 30 into 10 + 10 + 10, or 23 + 10 + 10 + 10 Count forward by 10s: 23, 33, 43, 53 23 + 30 = 53	**87 − 20** Break up 20 into 10 − 10, or 87 − 10 − 10 Count backward by 10s: 87, 77, 67 87 − 20 = 67

1. 42 + 20 = _____

2. 87 − 20 = _____

3. 63 − 30 = _____

4. 21 + 40 = _____

5. 50 + 30 = _____

6. 82 − 20 = _____

7. 42 + 40 = _____

8. 111 + 50 = _____

9. 133 − 30 = _____

10. 487 − 50 = _____

11. 599 − 60 = _____

12. 614 + 40 = _____

13. 832 + 30 = _____

14. 765 − 30 = _____

15. 1,425 + 50 = _____

16. 3,214 + 60 = _____

17. 5,555 − 50 = _____

18. 7,892 − 40 = _____

Write About It

Can you think of an even faster way to add or subtract tens numbers?

Breaking Up Numbers Is Easy to Do!

Directions: Solve each problem by breaking up numbers into easier numbers. Then regroup them for easier addition and subtraction. Look at the examples here.

Examples:

$32 + 47$ $= (30 + 2) + (40 + 7)$ $= (30 + 40) + (2 + 7)$ $= 70 + 9$ $= 79$	or	$32 + 47$ $= 32 + (40 + 7)$ $= (32 + 40) + 7$ $= 72 + 7$ $= 79$

$65 - 23$
$= 65 - 20 - 3$
$= 45 - 3$
$= 42$

1. $41 + 37 =$ _____

2. $86 + 13 =$ _____

3. $55 + 43 =$ _____

4. $23 + 15 =$ _____

5. $37 + 22 =$ _____

6. $74 + 25 =$ _____

7. $62 + 47 =$ _____

8. $46 + 43 =$ _____

9. $81 + 14 =$ _____

10. $64 + 35 =$ _____

11. $78 - 43 =$ _____

12. $65 - 32 =$ _____

13. $49 - 36 =$ _____

14. $56 - 25 =$ _____

15. $76 - 41 =$ _____

16. $59 - 36 =$ _____

17. $37 - 21 =$ _____

18. $45 - 24 =$ _____

19. $68 - 43 =$ _____

20. $87 - 62 =$ _____

MENTAL-MATH STRATEGIES: BREAKING UP NUMBERS

Breaking Up for Multiplication and Division

Directions: Solve each problem by breaking up numbers. Then regroup the numbers for easier multiplication and division. Look at the multiplication and division examples here.

Examples:

4×12	3×56	$36 \div 4$	$56 \div 4$
$= 4 \times (10 + 2)$	$= 3 \times (50 + 6)$	$= (20 + 16) \div 4$	$= (40 + 16) \div 4$
$= (4 \times 10) + (4 \times 2)$	$= (3 \times 50) + (3 \times 6)$	$= (20 \div 4) + (16 \div 4)$	$= (40 \div 4) + (16 \div 4)$
$= 40 + 8$	$= 150 + 18$	$= 5 + 4$	$= 10 + 4$
$= 48$	$= 168$	$= 9$	$= 14$

1. $3 \times 12 =$ _____

2. $5 \times 31 =$ _____

3. $4 \times 62 =$ _____

4. $2 \times 43 =$ _____

5. $4 \times 24 =$ _____

6. $3 \times 18 =$ _____

7. $5 \times 36 =$ _____

8. $8 \times 13 =$ _____

9. $7 \times 24 =$ _____

10. $6 \times 36 =$ _____

11. $24 \div 4 =$ _____

12. $35 \div 5 =$ _____

13. $48 \div 8 =$ _____

14. $56 \div 7 =$ _____

15. $26 \div 2 =$ _____

16. $48 \div 4 =$ _____

17. $75 \div 5 =$ _____

18. $96 \div 8 =$ _____

19. $64 \div 4 =$ _____

20. $60 \div 5 =$ _____

Write About It

Explain what shortcuts you used for one of the problems.

_____

MENTAL-MATH STRATEGIES: COMPENSATION

10 Is a Friend!

Directions: Solve the problems below by using compensation. Make tens to help you solve each problem. To make a ten, subtract from one number and add it to the other. Look at the examples below.

Here are some number combinations for which a ten can easily be made:

8 (+2) ⟶ 10	9 (+1) ⟶ 10	7 (−2) ⟶ 5
+ 5 (−2) ⟶ + 3	+ 7 (−1) ⟶ + 6	+ 8 (+2) ⟶ + 10
13	16	15

1.   9
      + 8
    _____

2.   4
      + 7
    _____

3.   6
      + 8
    _____

4.   4
      + 9
    _____

5.   6
      + 7
    _____

6.   4
      + 8
    _____

7.   9
      + 6
    _____

8.   7
      + 5
    _____

9.   3
      + 8
    _____

10.   9
      + 5
    _____

MENTAL-MATH STRATEGIES: COMPENSATION

9 Is Fine!

Look at the numbers
being added below:

Examples:

$$\begin{array}{r} 9 \\ +③ \\ \hline 1② \end{array} \qquad \begin{array}{r} 9 \\ +⑤ \\ \hline 1④ \end{array} \qquad \begin{array}{r} ⑧ \\ + 9 \\ \hline 1⑦ \end{array} \qquad \begin{array}{r} ④ \\ + 9 \\ \hline 1③ \end{array}$$

What do you notice about the
number being added to 9 and
the ones-place digit in the
answer? Make up a rule for
adding 9 to a number and
write it in the rule box at right.

Here's My Rule

Directions: Complete problems
1–5 by filling in the ones-place digit in the circle.
In problems 6–10, solve the problems using your new rule.

1. $\begin{array}{r} 9 \\ + 6 \\ \hline 1\bigcirc \end{array}$ 　　 2. $\begin{array}{r} 2 \\ + 9 \\ \hline 1\bigcirc \end{array}$ 　　 3. $\begin{array}{r} 9 \\ + 4 \\ \hline 1\bigcirc \end{array}$ 　　 4. $\begin{array}{r} 7 \\ + 9 \\ \hline 1\bigcirc \end{array}$ 　　 5. $\begin{array}{r} 9 \\ + 9 \\ \hline 1\bigcirc \end{array}$

6. $\begin{array}{r} 9 \\ + 5 \\ \hline \end{array}$ 　　 7. $\begin{array}{r} 9 \\ + 3 \\ \hline \end{array}$ 　　 8. $\begin{array}{r} 9 \\ + 8 \\ \hline \end{array}$ 　　 9. $\begin{array}{r} 2 \\ + 9 \\ \hline \end{array}$ 　　 10. $\begin{array}{r} 4 \\ + 9 \\ \hline \end{array}$

Name _____

Strategies for Adding 9 to a Number

Ms. Sousa: Adding **9** to a number is really simple.
Tyrone: Really, Ms. Sousa? Tell me more about it.
Ms. Sousa: OK, Tyrone. Watch what I write on the board. All of these examples can be done mentally.

27 + 9 = 36
483 + 9 = 492
756 + 9 = 765

Lattifa: Oh! Oh! Ms. Sousa, I see what you did to add those numbers quickly and mentally!

Ms. Sousa: Great, Lattifa! Please explain what you think I did.
Lattifa: You added **10** to the **27** and then took **1** away. You did the same thing with the others—you added **10** and subtracted **1**.
Juan: I just did the endings. For example, with **27** and **9**, I add the **7** and **9** and I know it is **16**. I keep the **6** and then jump to the next tens number, which is a **3**. That gives me **36**.
Ms. Sousa: Very good! Both strategies work beautifully.

Directions: Add 9 to the numbers below. Write your answers in the space.

1.	14 _____	8.	206 _____	15.	6,286 _____
2.	28 _____	9.	417 _____	16.	7,647 _____
3.	37 _____	10.	525 _____	17.	5,235 _____
4.	45 _____	11.	874 _____	18.	5,514 _____
5.	66 _____	12.	982 _____	19.	4,458 _____
6.	83 _____	13.	1,863 _____	20.	1,303 _____
7.	97 _____	14.	2,444 _____		

Write About It

Explain the strategy you used to solve the problems.

Easy Numbers Make Happy Faces!

Directions: Look at the addition problems below. See how you can make easy numbers by subtracting from one number and adding the same amount to the other? On the next page, fill in the eyes in the happy faces with easier numbers. Then solve the problems and write the correct answers in the space next to the happy face.

Add: 13 + 9

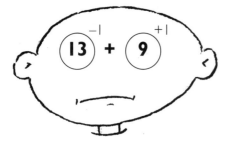 = 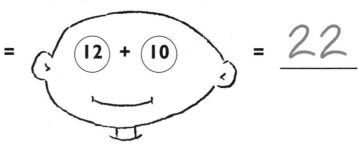 = **22**

Subtract 1 from 13 and add it to 9 to make 10.

12 + 10 is easier! The answer is 22.

Add: 12 + 36

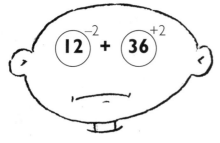 = 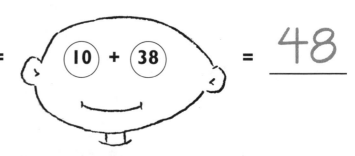 = **48**

Subtract 2 from 12 to make 10, and add it to 36.

10 + 38 is easier! The answer is 48.

(Continued on next page)

COMPENSATION

Easy Numbers Make Happy Faces!

1. (46 + 19) = (45 + ◯) = _____

2. (21 + 63) = (◯ + 64) = _____

3. (23 + 44) = (20 + ◯) = _____

4. (72 + 21) = (◯ + ◯) = _____

5. (67 + 12) = (◯ + ◯) = _____

6. (14 + 81) = (◯ + ◯) = _____

VISUALIZING NUMBERS & PATTERNS

Train Your Eyes to Memorize

Directions: Look at the first number below for about 4 seconds. Then cover it with your hand or a piece of paper. In the blanks next to the number, write the number you remember seeing. Do the same for the rest of the numbers. Do only one number at a time.

347	___ ___ ___
439	___ ___ ___
3,621	___ ___ ___ ___
5,556	___ ___ ___ ___
13,579	___ ___ ___ ___ ___
87,592	___ ___ ___ ___ ___
37,738	___ ___ ___ ___ ___
69,971	___ ___ ___ ___ ___
132,156	___ ___ ___ ___ ___ ___
261,008	___ ___ ___ ___ ___ ___
402,619	___ ___ ___ ___ ___ ___
796,215	___ ___ ___ ___ ___ ___

On Your Own

Repeat the activity, except this time write the numbers backward.

Write About It

What numbers do you use almost every day that you have to memorize?

_____

_____

_____

_____

One-Hundred Chart

1	2	3	4	5	6	7	8	9	10
11	12	13	14	15	16	17	18	19	20
21	22	23	24	25	26	27	28	29	30
31	32	33	34	35	36	37	38	39	40
41	42	43	44	45	46	47	48	49	50
51	52	53	54	55	56	57	58	59	60
61	62	63	64	65	66	67	68	69	70
71	72	73	74	75	76	77	78	79	80
81	82	83	84	85	86	87	88	89	90
91	92	93	94	95	96	97	98	99	100

VISUALIZING NUMBERS & PATTERNS

Patterns in the One-Hundred Chart

Directions: Use the One-Hundred Chart on page 21 to answer the questions below.

1. Notice that the first row contains numbers ending in 1, 2, 3, 4, 5, 6, 7, 8, 9, and 0. Does the second row have the same pattern? What about row 3? What about each of the remaining rows?

_____

2. Look at the first column. What number appears in each number in the column? Is there a pattern in the column?

_____

3. Look at the second column. What number appears in each number in the column?

_____

4. Are there even-number columns and odd-number columns? Which ones are even? Which ones are odd?

_____

5. If you count by twos starting with 2, are the numbers you count odd or even? What if you started with 3 and counted by twos? Are the numbers you count odd or even?

6. Look at the chart diagonally, going from 1 to 12 to 23, etc. What pattern do you see?

_____

7. Look at the column that starts with 8. From there, count by 10s. For example: 8, 18, 28. How much more is the number below any given number on the chart? Why would you say that counting downward is like counting by 10s? What about counting upward?

_____

8. Starting with 5, count nine spaces more. What number do you land on? Continue to the end of the chart. What pattern do you notice?

_____

9. Starting with 8, count nine spaces more. What number do you land on? Continue to the end of the chart. What pattern do you notice?

_____

10. Find all of the double-digit numbers, such as 11, 22, 33. What pattern do they make?

_____

Write About It

Of all the patterns that you have seen on the One-Hundred Chart, which one interests you the most?

_____

VISUALIZING NUMBERS & PATTERNS

Follow the Pattern

Directions: Look at the numbers in each column below. Can you figure out the pattern? Complete each column, using what you remember of the One-Hundred Chart.

2	10	5	8	4
12	20	15	18	14

Name _____

VISUALIZING NUMBERS & PATTERNS

No Looking! What's Missing?

Directions: Use what you remember of the One-Hundred Chart to fill in the squares below with the correct numbers. Look at the example here.

Example:

43	44	45

51	52	53

1.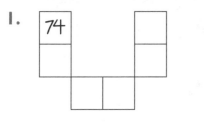

7.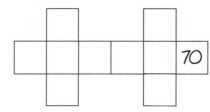

2.

8.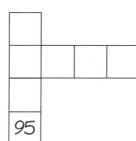

3.

4.

9.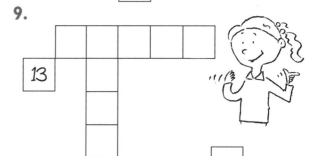

5.

10.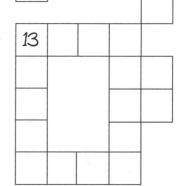

6.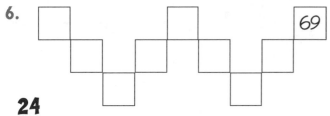

24

Name _____

After and Before Numbers

> **Directions:** Use mental math and your knowledge of the One-Hundred Chart to solve the problems below.

What number comes

1. 1 after 20? _____
2. 2 after 44? _____
3. 3 after 52? _____
4. 4 after 34? _____
5. 5 after 67? _____
6. 2 after 75? _____
7. 4 after 91? _____
8. 6 after 80? _____
9. 8 after 96? _____
10. 9 after 100? _____
11. 3 after 50? _____
12. 5 after 25? _____
13. 7 after 87? _____
14. 9 after 61? _____
15. 8 after 97? _____
16. 3 after 72? _____
17. 5 after 87? _____
18. 7 after 53? _____
19. 8 after 94? _____
20. 10 after 100? _____

What number comes

21. 3 before 5? _____
22. 2 before 8? _____
23. 5 before 12? _____
24. 10 before 15? _____
25. 2 before 22? _____
26. 2 before 18? _____
27. 8 before 38? _____
28. 5 before 30? _____
29. 7 before 49? _____
30. 1 before 51? _____
31. 5 before 76? _____
32. 4 before 50? _____
33. 3 before 63? _____
34. 5 before 72? _____
35. 4 before 88? _____
36. 8 before 68? _____
37. 7 before 70? _____
38. 9 before 81? _____
39. 6 before 95? _____
40. 10 before 98? _____

Write About It

How did you use mental math to figure out the number that comes 8 after 96?

_____

_____

_____

_____

VISUALIZING NUMBERS & PATTERNS

Skip to My 2s

Directions: List the next five numbers in each pattern below. Count by 2s. We started the first one for you.

1. **2, 4, 6,** _8_ , _10_ , ____, ____, ____

2. **20, 22, 24,** ____, ____, ____, ____, ____

3. **42, 44, 46,** ____, ____, ____, ____, ____

4. **74, 76, 78,** ____, ____, ____, ____, ____

5. **98, 100, 102,** ____, ____, ____, ____, ____

6. **3, 5, 7,** ____, ____, ____, ____, ____

7. **21, 23, 25,** ____, ____, ____, ____, ____

8. **53, 55, 57,** ____, ____, ____, ____, ____

9. **79, 81, 83,** ____, ____, ____, ____, ____

10. **97, 99, 101,** ____, ____, ____, ____, ____

VISUALIZING NUMBERS & PATTERNS

Skip to My 2s

. . . BACKWARD!

> **Directions:** List the next five numbers in each pattern below. Count backward by 2s. We started the first one for you.

1. 16, 14, 12, _10_, _8_, ____, ____, ____

2. 40, 38, 36, ____, ____, ____, ____, ____

3. 88, 86, 84, ____, ____, ____, ____, ____

4. 100, 98, 96, ____, ____, ____, ____, ____

5. 108, 106, 104, ____, ____, ____, ____, ____

6. 150, 148, 146, ____, ____, ____, ____, ____

7. 17, 15, 13, ____, ____, ____, ____, ____

8. 21, 19, 17, ____, ____, ____, ____, ____

9. 37, 35, 33, ____, ____, ____, ____, ____

10. 65, 63, 61, ____, ____, ____, ____, ____

Name _____

VISUALIZING NUMBERS & PATTERNS

Ladders and Chutes

Directions: Count by 10s to climb the ladders and slide down the chutes.

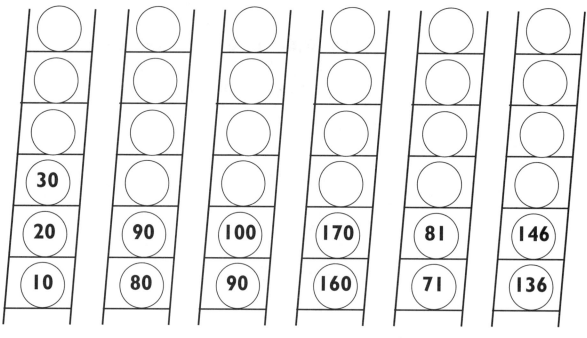

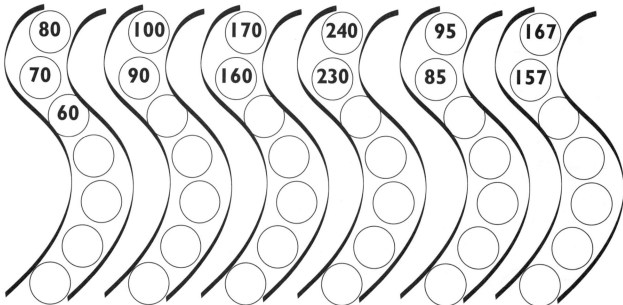

28

VISUALIZING NUMBERS & PATTERNS

Follow the Winding Brick Road!

Directions: Look at the winding roads below. Each one increases or decreases by 25 or 50. Fill in the spaces in each road.

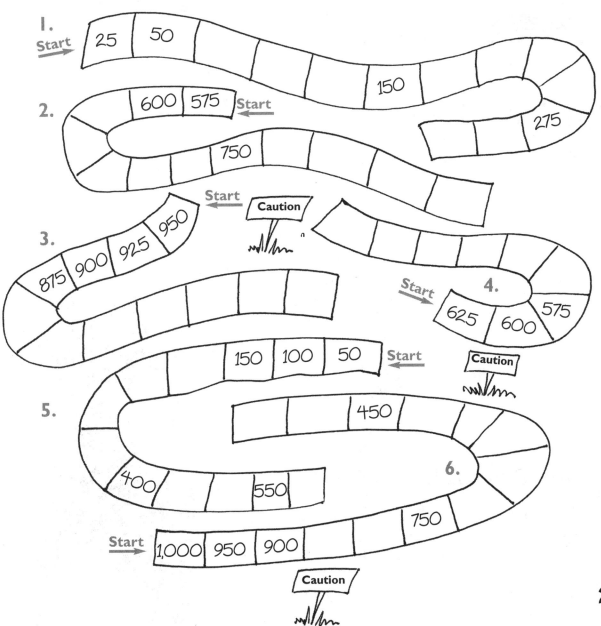

1. Start → 25 | 50 | | | | | 150 | | | | 275

2. | 600 | 575 | ← Start | | | | | 750 | | | |

3. 950 | 925 | 900 | 875 | Start ← Caution

4. Start → 625 | 600 | 575 | Caution

5. 150 | 100 | 50 | ← Start | 450 | 400 | 550 | 750

Start → 1,000 | 950 | 900 | Caution

6.

29

Name _____

VISUALIZING NUMBERS & PATTERNS

Lucky 7

Directions: There are 19 numbers between 0 and 100 that have a 7 in them. List all of those numbers below.

1. _____   2. _____   3. _____

4. _____

5. _____

6. _____

7. _____

8. _____

9. _____

10. _____

11. _____   12. _____   13. _____

14. _____

15. _____

16. _____

17. _____

18. _____

19. _____

Write About It

How many 7s in all did you find?

VISUALIZING NUMBERS & PATTERNS

Getting to the Price Is Right

Do this activity with a classmate. With your partner, study the shopping list below. Next to each item, you'll find its cost. Take the list and test your partner to see if he or she remembers the cost of each item.

Ask: How much does the TV set cost? Let your partner keep guessing the price until getting the correct answer. Help your partner by saying whether the guess is lower or higher than the answer.

Let the exchange continue until your partner gives the correct answer. Then move on to the next item. When you've gone through the entire list, work with your partner to change the price of each item. Then, give your partner the list and switch places.

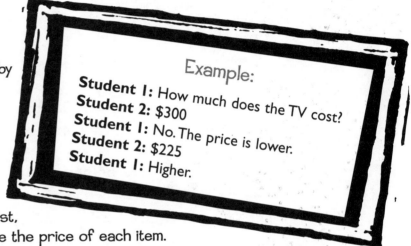

Example:
Student 1: How much does the TV cost?
Student 2: $300
Student 1: No. The price is lower.
Student 2: $225
Student 1: Higher.

TV set
$268.00

Crayon set
$3.25

1 gallon of gas
$1.41

1 gallon of milk
$2.79

Bar of soap
$2.19

Sneakers
$24.95

1-pound jar of peanut butter
$2.49

Sweater
$13.50

Name _____

Doubles Are No Trouble!

Directions: Find the sums of the doubled numbers below.

1. 5 + 5 = _____   4. 3 + 3 = _____   7. 8 + 8 = _____

2. 2 + 2 = _____   5. 1 + 1 = _____   8. 6 + 6 = _____

3. 7 + 7 = _____   6. 4 + 4 = _____   9. 9 + 9 = _____

Fold your paper here before doing the exercises below.

- -

The sums below are the results of doubled numbers.
Fill in the blanks with the doubled numbers.

11.

10. _____ + _____ = 8   _____ + _____ = 4

12. _____ + _____ = 18   13. _____ + _____ = 10

14. _____ + _____ = 16   15. _____ + _____ = 6

16. _____ + _____ = 2   17. _____ + _____ = 14

18. _____ + _____ = 12

Name _____

NUMBER FACTS

Double the Number, Double the Fun!

Directions: Follow the arrows and double each number as you move along. We did the first one for you.

1. 2 → 4 → 8

2. ○ ← ○ ← 9

3. ○ ← ○ ← 7

4. 8 → ○ → ○

5. ○ ↑ ○ ↑ 1

6. 10 → ○ → ○

7. ○ ← ○ ← 5

8. ○ ← ○ ← 6 →

9. ○ ← ○ ← 3

10. ○ ← ○ ← 4 →

NUMBER FACTS

E-Z Strategy Using Doubles

Did you ever try to remember the answer to 8 + 7 and couldn't remember what it was? Here is a strategy that can help you remember the answer:

Use doubles to help learn other facts. For example: use **6 + 6 = 12** to help learn **6 + 7 = 13** and **6 + 5 = 11**.

If you know that **6 + 6 = 12**, then it's easy to figure out that **6 + 7 = 13** because 7 is one more than 6.

You'll also know that **6 + 5 = 11** because 5 is one less than 6.

Directions: Solve each problem below.

1. 8 + 8 = _____
   8 + 9 = _____
   8 + 7 = _____

2. 7 + 7 = _____
   7 + 6 = _____
   7 + 8 = _____

3. 5 + 5 = _____
   5 + 6 = _____
   5 + 4 = _____

4. 9 + 9 = _____
   9 + 8 = _____
   9 + 10 = _____

5. 6 + 6 = _____
   6 + 5 = _____
   6 + 7 = _____

6. 10 + 10 = _____
   10 + 11 = _____
   10 + 9 = _____

NUMBER FACTS

You Can Half It!

Directions: Answer the questions below.

1. **What is half of 4?**

_____

2. **What is half of 6?**

_____

3. **What is half of 10?**

_____

4. **What is half of 20?**

_____

5. **What is half of 60?**

6. **What is half of 80?**

_____

7. **What is half of 100?**

_____

8. **What is half of 400?**

_____

9. **What is half of 600?**

_____

10. **What is half of 800?**

_____

NUMBER FACTS

How Many Beans Are in the Pot?

Say there are 4 beans in the first pot. There are a total of 7 beans. How many beans are in the second pot below? Figure out what's in the second pot by looking at this drawing:

$$\boxed{4} \quad + \quad \boxed{?} \quad = \quad 7$$

Did you figure out the answer? Here's a strategy we used:

Subtract the number of beans in the first pot from the total number of beans (7 − 4). The answer is the number of beans in the second pot (7 − 4 = 3).
So, there are 3 beans in the second pot.

Directions: How many beans are in the blank pots below? Fill in the correct number of beans in each pot.

1. $\boxed{2} + \boxed{} = 7$

2. $\boxed{} + \boxed{4} = 9$

3. $\boxed{6} + \boxed{} = 11$

4. $\boxed{} + \boxed{7} = 12$

5. $\boxed{} + \boxed{9} = 16$

6. $\boxed{8} + \boxed{} = 17$

7. $\boxed{5} + \boxed{} = 13$

8. $\boxed{7} + \boxed{} = 14$

9. $\boxed{} + \boxed{9} = 12$

10. $\boxed{6} + \boxed{} = 13$

NUMBER FACTS

What's the Missing Number?

Directions: Find the missing number to complete each addition fact. See the example below.

Example:

> When you see 3, 4, 7, think 3 + 4 = 7.
> So when you see 3, ___, 7, think 3 +___ = 7.
> The missing number is 4.

1. 5, _____, 10

2. 4, _____, 6

3. 5, _____, 8

4. 6, _____, 10

5. _____, 7, 9

6. 4, _____, 12

7. _____, 8, 12

8. 9, _____, 12

9. 5, _____, 12

10. 3, _____, 12

11. 8, _____, 15

12. 6, _____, 14

13. _____, 7, 15

14. 4, _____, 11

15. _____, 6, 15

16. 8, _____, 13

17. _____, 9, 18

18. 5, _____, 14

19. _____, 7, 13

20. 8, _____, 17

NUMBER FACTS

It's All in the Number Family

Directions: Write in the missing three family members for each equation below. Before you start, look at the examples.

Examples:

Here is the number family for 3 + 4 = 7:	Here is the number family for 9 + 5 = 14:
3 + 4 = 7	9 + 5 = 14
4 + 3 = 7	5 + 9 = 14
7 − 3 = 4	14 − 9 = 5
7 − 4 = 3	14 − 5 = 9

1. 5 + 4 = 9

_____

_____

4. _____

_____

13 − 7 = 6

_____

7. 9 + 7 = 16

_____

_____

10. _____

_____

15 − 8 = 7

2. 3 + 8 = 11

_____

_____

5. _____

_____

_____

12 − 4 = 8

8. _____

_____

15 − 9 = 6

_____

11. 8 + 5 = 13

_____

_____

3. 4 + 6 = 10

_____

_____

6. 6 + 5 = 11

_____

_____

9. 7 + 6 = 13

_____

_____

12. _____

_____

11 − 4 = 7

_____

+/- Flash Cards

Here's an addition-and-
subtraction flash card:

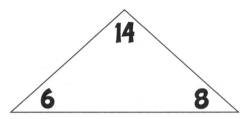

The number at the top of the
triangle is the sum of the two
numbers along the bottom of the
triangle: 14 = 6 + 8

Directions: Complete the triangles below by filling in the missing
number. Notice that some of the triangles are upside down.

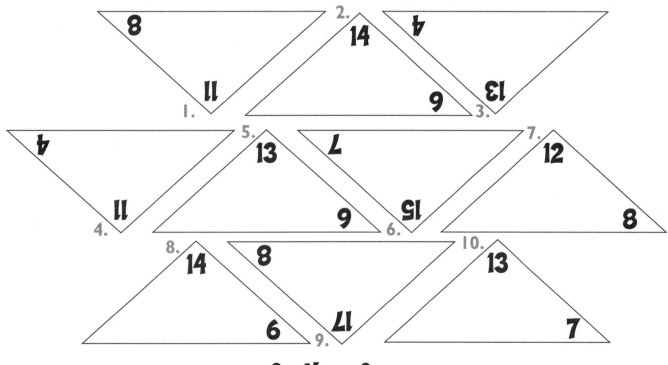

On Your Own

When you've finished filling in the missing number, cut out the triangles, including
the sample above. For more addition practice, cover the top number of a completed
triangle with your thumb. Have a classmate guess the number hidden by your
thumb. For subtraction practice, cover one of the corner numbers, and have a
classmate guess the hidden number.

x/÷ Flash Cards

Here's a multiplication-and-division flash card:

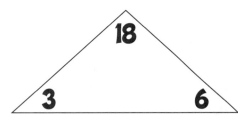

The number at the top of the triangle is the product of the two numbers along the bottom: 18 = 3 x 6.

The number in either the left corner or right corner of the triangle is the quotient of the number at the top of the triangle divided by the number at the other corner: 18 ÷ 3 = 6 and 18 ÷ 6 = 3.

Directions: Complete the triangles below by filling in the missing number. Notice that some of the triangles are upside down.

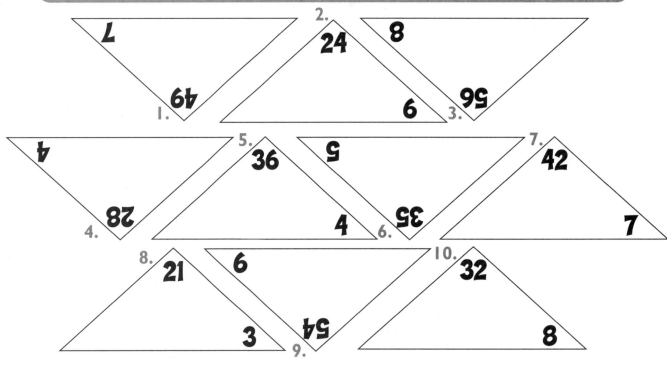

On Your Own

When you've finished filling in the missing number, cut out the triangles, including the sample above. For more multiplication practice, cover the top number of a completed triangle with your thumb. Have a classmate guess the number hidden by your thumb. For division practice, cover one of the corner numbers, and have a classmate guess the hidden number.

Name _____

NUMBER FACTS

Don't Carry That 10!

Say you're adding a one-digit number, like 5, to a two-digit number, like 27. You probably add the ones column first, then carry over to the tens column. Try this mental-math strategy of jumping to the next 10 instead:

Take 27 + 5:

First, add 7 + 5 = 12. Instead of 12, think 2 (the ones column).
Then, think of the next 10s: 20 ——▶ 30. The final answer is 32.

Directions: Mentally add the number inside the circle to each of the numbers outside. Instead of carrying over, jump to the next 10s.

1.

4.

2.

5.

3.

6.

NUMBER FACTS

Adding 100s And 1,000s

Directions: Add 100 to each of the numbers below. Write the answers in the spaces. We did the first one for you.

1.	32	_132_		11.	900	_____
2.	42	_____		12.	2,614	_____
3.	67	_____		13.	1,405	_____
4.	100	_____		14.	8,888	_____
5.	107	_____		15.	5,421	_____
6.	313	_____		16.	5,015	_____
7.	601	_____		17.	4,900	_____
8.	728	_____		18.	3,027	_____
9.	899	_____		19.	1,111	_____
10.	524	_____		20.	6,490	_____

Add 1,000 to each of the numbers below.

21.	37	_____
22.	195	_____
23.	440	_____
24.	99	_____
25.	457	_____
26.	53	

Add 2,000 to each of the numbers below.

27.	4,516	_____
28.	5,041	_____
29.	6,507	_____
30.	3,007	_____
31.	1,234	_____
32.	3,773	_____

Name _____

NUMBER FACTS

Hit the Target Number

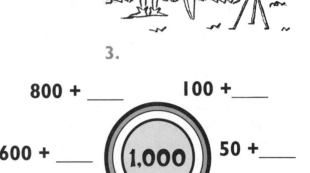

Directions: Look at the target number in each bull's-eye. Then fill in the blank with the missing number that will add up to the target number. See the example:

Example:

50 + _50_

30 + _70_   **100**   10 + _90_

45 + _55_

3.

800 + ____   100 + ____

600 + ____   **1,000**   50 + ____

550 + ____   300 + ____

1.

200 + ____   100 + ____

250 + ____   **300**   125 + ____

150 + ____   50 + ____

4.

800 + ____

825 + ____

750 + ____   **850**   600 + ____

725 + ____   700 + ____

2.

100 + ____   300 + ____

450 + ____   **500**   425 + ____

350 + ____   475 + ____

5.

690 + ____   600 + ____

680 + ____   **692**   686 + ____

650 + ____   675 + ____

43

NUMBER FACTS

Subtracting From 100 Is Easy!

Brian: I wish there were an easy way to subtract numbers from 100.

Bella: There is!

Brian: Really?

Bella: Yes, and I can teach it to you in a minute!

Brian: How are you going to do that?

Bella: There's a pattern. Let me show you. I'll write some problems on the board. See if you can find the pattern.

Examples:			
100 − 38	100 − 53	100 − 86	100 − 24
62	47	14	76

$3 + ? = 9$

$8 + ? = 10$

Brian: I see part of the pattern. For the tens-place number, you think 3 plus what number makes 9. The answer is 6. But how do you get the ones-place number so quickly?

Bella: Easy! Just think 8 plus what number makes 10. The answer is 2.

Brian: Wait, Bella. Let me do the next example. For the tens digit, 5 plus what number makes 9? The answer is 4. Then, for the ones digit, 3 plus what number makes 10? The answer is 7. The final answer then is 4 and 7, or 47.

Bella: Does the pattern work for the next two examples?

Brian: It sure does! See for yourself.

Write About It

Explain how Brian got 14 for the third problem and 76 for the last problem.

_____

NUMBER FACTS

Subtracting From 100 Is Easy – Part 2

Directions: Use the pattern strategy from page 44 to solve the subtraction problems below.

1.   100
   − 43
	5. 100
	   − 35
		9. 100
		   − 71

2.   100
   − 51
	6. 100
	   − 22
		10. 100
		   − 58

3.   100
   − 87
	7. 100
	   − 17
		11. 100
		   − 26

4.   100
   − 68
	8. 100
	   − 39
		12. 100
		   − 77

Name _____

SKILL BUILDERS

Pick a Pair of Pears

Directions: Fill in the blanks with a number from a pear at right. You can use each number more than once.

1. 15 + _____ = 25   8. _____ + _____ = 80

2. 16 + _____ = 46   9. _____ + _____ = 60

3. 5 + _____ = 75   10. _____ + _____ = 100

4. _____ + 30 = 40   11. _____ + _____ = 100

5. _____ + 43 = 93   12. _____ + _____ = 120

6. 31 + _____ = 61   13. _____ + _____ = 120

7. 29 + _____ = 79   14. _____ + _____ = 160

Write About It

Tell why it's impossible to pick 2 pears to make 75.

46 _____

Number Chain Links

Directions: Follow the numbers and signs on each chain link, then write the correct answer in the last, empty link.

1. (4)=(+)=(2)=(+)=(5)=(–)=(2)=(=)=(*9*)

2. (3)=(+)=(2)=(+)=(4)=(–)=(7)=(=)=( )

3. (10)=(–)=(6)=(+)=(4)=(–)=(2)=(=)=( )

4. (10)=(+)=(20)=(+)=(5)=(–)=(10)=(=)=( )

5. (15)=(–)=(7)=(+)=(8)=(+)=(4)=(=)=( )

6. (25)=(–)=(5)=(+)=(10)=(–)=(8)=(=)=( )

7. (40)=(–)=(8)=(–)=(2)=(–)=(10)=(=)=( )

8. (80)=(+)=(20)=(+)=(200)=(+)=(300)=(=)=( )

On Your Own

On a separate sheet of paper, make your own number chain links.

SKILL BUILDERS

Follow the Finger

Directions: Practice addition and subtraction with the following activity: Point to one of the numbers in the chart below. Then, point to either the plus sign or the minus sign. Next, point to a second number in the chart. What's the answer? For example, point to the number 4. Then, point to the plus sign. Now, point to the number 3. You've created the problem 4 + 3. The answer is 7.

4	1	8	5	7
9	3	6	0	2

(+)   (-)

On Your Own

Make this activity more challenging by adding or subtracting more than three numbers. You can also replace the plus and minus signs with the multiplication (x) and division (÷) signs.

Name _____

Mental Math Can Save Time

$$100 + 50 + 50 = 200$$

Directions: Which of the problems below can you solve in your head? Circle the ones you can do mentally, and then write in the answers.

1.	$\begin{array}{r} 100 \\ -\ 1 \\ \hline \end{array}$	5.	$\begin{array}{r} 150 \\ +151 \\ \hline \end{array}$	9.	$\begin{array}{r} 100 \\ 400 \\ +300 \\ \hline \end{array}$	13.	$\begin{array}{r} 100 \\ -\ 20 \\ \hline \end{array}$
2.	$\begin{array}{r} 99 \\ +\ 1 \\ \hline \end{array}$	6.	$\begin{array}{r} 1{,}000 \\ -\ 300 \\ \hline \end{array}$	10.	$\begin{array}{r} 400 \\ +\ 5 \\ \hline \end{array}$	14.	$\begin{array}{r} 100 \\ -\ 50 \\ \hline \end{array}$
3.	$\begin{array}{r} 92 \\ +\ 2 \\ \hline \end{array}$	7.	$\begin{array}{r} 100 \\ -\ 90 \\ \hline \end{array}$	11.	$\begin{array}{r} 100 \\ -\ 60 \\ \hline \end{array}$	15.	$\begin{array}{r} 50 \\ +\ 50 \\ \hline \end{array}$
4.	$\begin{array}{r} 98 \\ +\ 2 \\ \hline \end{array}$	8.	$\begin{array}{r} 100 \\ +\ 44 \\ \hline \end{array}$	12.	$\begin{array}{r} 125 \\ +\ 25 \\ \hline \end{array}$	16.	$\begin{array}{r} 1{,}000 \\ -\ 200 \\ \hline \end{array}$

Write About It

Explain how you solved problem #16 mentally.

_____

_____

Letters Have Values, Too!

Directions: The chart here gives number values to letters. Use the chart to figure out the value of the words listed below.

Example:

f a c e

f = 25, a = 10, c = 50, e = 100

Add the numbers in your head. One way is to add numbers to make easy numbers: 25 + 50 = 75. Then, add 10: 75 + 10 = 85. Finally, add 100: 85 + 100 = 185. Or, you can add the numbers from largest to smallest to get the answer: 100 + 50 + 25 + 10 = 185.

Letter	Number Value
a	10
b	25
c	50
d	10
e	100
f	25
g	50

	Word	Value		Word	Value
1.	fad	_____	11.	gab	_____
2.	add	_____	12.	fee	_____
3.	ebb	_____	13.	bag	_____
4.	fade	_____	14.	dead	_____
5.	ace	_____	15.	gag	_____
6.	cad	_____	16.	feed	_____
7.	deaf	_____	17.	dad	_____
8.	fed	_____	18.	bee	_____
9.	café	_____	19.	cab	_____
10.	deed	_____	20.	bad	_____

On Your Own

Make up your own letter-values activity on a separate sheet of paper. Remember to use numbers that can easily be added mentally.

Name _____

Calculate on Your Calculator

Directions: Look at how the number changes in each box. Circle the plus or minus sign to show whether you add or subtract to get the new number. Finally, write the number that you add or subtract to get the new number in the space. Look at the example below.

Example: **To change** 346 **to** 376 **,**

(+) / – ___30___

1. **To change** 346 **to** 347 **,**
   + / – _____

2. **To change** 632 **to** 652 **,**
   + / – _____

3. **To change** 9876 **to** 9976 **,**
   + / – _____

4. **To change** 5123 **to** 5103 **,**
   + / – _____

5. **To change** 3778 **to** 1778 **,**
   + / – _____

6. **To change** 4295 **to** 7295 **,**
   + / – _____

7. **To change** 1243 **to** 1249 **,**
   + / – _____

8. **To change** 6820 **to** 6880 **,**
   + / – _____

9. **To change** 9876 **to** 9800 **,**
   + / – _____

10. **To change** 4378 **to** 4078 **,**
    + / – _____

Write About It

Explain how you solved problem #9.

Name _____

Exercise Your Number Sense

Directions: Change each number below by mentally adding and subtracting. We did the first one for you. Finish one column completely before you move on to the next.

	+ 10	– 10	+ 5	– 5	+ 9	– 9	+ 11	– 11	+ 100	+ 99	+ 1,000
24	34	14	29	19	33	15	35	13	124	123	1,024
82											
51											
17											
90											
105											
130											
165											
392											
499											

Write About It

What strategy did you use to find the answer to 90 minus 11?

_____

_____

Name _____

SKILL BUILDERS

Circle the Largest Answer

> **Directions:** For each number, circle the equation with the largest answer. You should be able to explain why you chose your answer.

1. 35 + 1
   35 + 0
   35 + 2

2. 13 – 6
   13 – 5
   13 – 7

3. 145 – 6
   145 – 16
   145 + 0

4. 18 + 5
   19 + 5
   17 + 5

5. 25 + 5 + 4
   25 + 10
   25 + 2 + 3

6. 100 – 10
   100 – 20
   100 – 30

7. 20 + 30
   20 + 40
   20 + 20

8. 100 + 30
   100 + 20
   100 + 40

9. 95 + 5
   100 – 0
   11 + 90

10. 1,000 + 50
    1,000 – 50
    1,000 – 100

53

Name _____

The Largest Number in a Diamond

Directions: Look at the problems and numbers in each diamond below. Circle the one that has the largest answer. Remember to solve the problems using mental math.

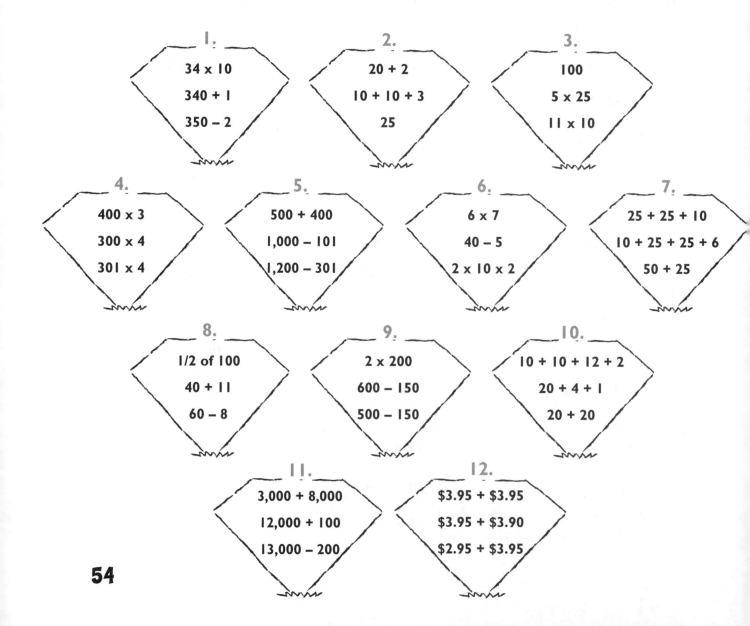

1.
34 x 10
340 + 1
350 – 2

2.
20 + 2
10 + 10 + 3
25

3.
100
5 x 25
11 x 10

4.
400 x 3
300 x 4
301 x 4

5.
500 + 400
1,000 – 101
1,200 – 301

6.
6 x 7
40 – 5
2 x 10 x 2

7.
25 + 25 + 10
10 + 25 + 25 + 6
50 + 25

8.
1/2 of 100
40 + 11
60 – 8

9.
2 x 200
600 – 150
500 – 150

10.
10 + 10 + 12 + 2
20 + 4 + 1
20 + 20

11.
3,000 + 8,000
12,000 + 100
13,000 – 200

12.
$3.95 + $3.95
$3.95 + $3.90
$2.95 + $3.95

54

In Your Estimation ...

> **Directions:** Use estimation to solve the problems below.

1. **Circle the examples that have answers greater than 100.**

   a. 4 x 50   d. 342 − 200

   b. 505 ÷ 5   e. 8 x 12

   c. 10 x 12

2. **Circle the examples that have answers greater than 2,000.**

   a. 543 + 678 + 925   d. 872 + 100 + 562 + 129

   b. 1,256 + 324   e. 3,215 − 1,214

   c. 5,000 − 4,125

3. **Write the number of digits (not the actual answer) that would be in the answer for each problem in the blank.**

   a. 25 + 50 + 975 _____   d. 25 + 50 + 25 _____

   b. 345 + 50 + 692 _____   e. 3,000 − 275 _____

   c. (3 x 50) + 25 _____   f. 5,000 − 4,526 _____

4. **Circle the plus sign if the estimated answer is an over-estimate. Circle the minus sign if the estimated answer is an underestimate.**

Problem	Estimated Answer	Over	Under
a. 4 x 39	120	+	−
b. 501 x 4	2,000	+	−
c. 648 + 250	1,000	+	−
d. 4,325 − 2,951	1,000	+	−

SKILL BUILDERS

Shape Up With Numbers!

Directions: Fill in the geometric shapes with numbers that will make each equation correct. In each problem, a shape stands for the same number in both equations. See the example below.

Example:

$$\triangle + \bigcirc = 12$$

$$\triangle - \bigcirc = 2$$

The numbers that solve the first equation are the same numbers that solve the second equation:

$$7 + 5 = 12$$
$$7 - 5 = 2$$

1.
$$\square \times \triangle = 24$$
$$\square + \triangle = 11$$

4.
$$\bigcirc \times \triangle = 56$$
$$\bigcirc - \triangle = 1$$

7.
$$\bigcirc \times \square = 54$$
$$\bigcirc + \square = 15$$

2.
$$\square \times \bigcirc = 28$$
$$\square - \bigcirc = 3$$

5.
$$\triangle \times \square = 15$$
$$\triangle - \square = 2$$

8.
$$\triangledown \times \square = 32$$
$$\triangledown - \square = 4$$

3.
$$\bigcirc \times \bigcirc = 81$$
$$\bigcirc + \bigcirc = 18$$

6.
$$\square \times \square = 49$$
$$\square - \square = 0$$

9.
$$\bigcirc \times \square = 48$$
$$\bigcirc - \square = 2$$

Name _____

CONCENTRATION: Mental-Math Style

Directions: Play this game with a friend. First, cut out the cards below. Some cards contain problems, while others have answers to those problems. Place the cards facedown in three rows on a table. With players taking turns, flip over two cards. If you turn over a card with a problem and another card with its matching answer, you get to keep both cards. Take another turn. Otherwise, turn the cards facedown again and the other player takes a turn. Keep playing until no cards remain. The person with the most matching cards wins.

$(7 \times 6) + 5$	59	$(6 \times 6) + 3$	49
A	**B**	**C**	**D**
27	$(8 \times 5) + 9$	37	$(7 \times 7) + 2$
E	**F**	**G**	**H**
$(5 \times 4) + 7$	80	47	$(8 \times 9) + 8$
I	**J**	**K**	**L**
39	$(7 \times 4) + 9$	$(9 \times 6) + 5$	51
M	**N**	**O**	**P**

What's Left?

Directions: When you solve the division problems here, each will have a remainder that's equal to one of the numbers below. Write the **remainder** for each problem in the space provided.

Remainders
0 1 2 3 4

1. 7 ÷ 2 _____	11. 27 ÷ 5 _____	21. 24 ÷ 5 _____
2. 6 ÷ 3 _____	12. 15 ÷ 7 _____	22. 14 ÷ 7 _____
3. 10 ÷ 3 _____	13. 5 ÷ 2 _____	23. 6 ÷ 4 _____
4. 12 ÷ 5 _____	14. 16 ÷ 4 _____	24. 9 ÷ 4 _____
5. 12 ÷ 6 _____	15. 11 ÷ 2 _____	25. 5 ÷ 3 _____
6. 7 ÷ 3 _____	16. 10 ÷ 4 _____	26. 13 ÷ 5 _____
7. 14 ÷ 4 _____	17. 21 ÷ 5 _____	27. 30 ÷ 6 _____
8. 10 ÷ 5 _____	18. 10 ÷ 6 _____	28. 40 ÷ 6 _____
9. 20 ÷ 6 _____	19. 9 ÷ 9 _____	29. 15 ÷ 3 _____
10. 15 ÷ 6 _____	20. 12 ÷ 4 _____	30. 25 ÷ 6 _____

Name _____

What's Your Change?

Directions:

How much change will you get from $1.00 if you
spend 5¢ on a piece of bubble gum? _____

How much change will you get from $1.00 if you . . .

Spend	Change from $1.00	Spend	Change from $1.00
1. 10¢	_____	10. 50¢	_____
2. 80¢	_____	11. 25¢	_____
3. 75¢	_____	12. 20¢	_____
4. 98¢	_____	13. 99¢	_____
5. 90¢	_____	14. 94¢	_____
6. 8¢	_____	15. 91¢	_____
7. 85¢	_____	16. 60¢	_____
8. 30¢	_____	17. 61¢	_____
9. 15¢	_____	18. 40¢	_____

Write About It

Say you have $1.00. Would you get more or less change
if you spend 61¢ instead of 60¢? Explain your answer.

Name_____

MONEY MATH

How Much Is in the Piggy Bank?

Directions: Six students in Mrs. Ramon's class save money in a piggy bank. Below are the students' piggy banks. How much does each student have in his or her piggy bank? Write your answer in the blank.

Karen's piggy bank

_____

Thomas's piggy bank

_____

Alvin's piggy bank

_____

Rosita's piggy bank

_____

Ricky's piggy bank

_____

Marta's piggy bank

_____

60

Name _____

MONEY MATH

Calculator-Free Shopping

Directions: Below are items found in a grocery and their cost. Read each person's shopping list and use mental math to figure out how much each person spent.

Cereal
$2.00

Soda
$1.50

Milk
$1.25

Peanut butter
$1.50

Coffee
$3.00

Bread
$1.50

Chewing gum
$.25

Toothpaste
$2.50

Ken's Shopping List

2 liters of soda
1 carton of milk

Total cost:

Olivia's Shopping List

1 jar of peanut butter
1 box of cereal
1 can of coffee
1 loaf of bread

Total cost:

Annette's Shopping List

1 jar of peanut butter
1 box of cereal
1 carton of milk
1 loaf of bread

Total cost:

(Continued on next page)

Name _____

Calculator-Free Shopping

Bella's Shopping List

1 tube of toothpaste
1 carton of milk
1 box of cereal

Total cost:

_____

Todd's Shopping List

2 packs of chewing gum
2 liters of soda

Total cost:

_____

Marianne's Shopping List

2 boxes of cereal
2 cartons of milk

Total cost:

_____

Ben's Shopping List

2 liters of soda
2 packs of chewing gum
1 can of coffee

Total cost:

_____

Brian's Shopping List

3 cans of coffee
2 boxes of cereal
2 tubes of toothpaste

Total cost:

_____

Tucker's Shopping List

1 liter of soda
4 packs of chewing gum
1 jar of peanut butter

Total cost:

_____

Write About It

Explain how you figured out how much Brian spent at the supermarket.

_____

_____

Name _____

MONEY MATH

Who Has Enough Money?

> **Directions:** Each of the shoppers below has $25 to spend at a store. The store receipts show how much each person spent on the items he or she bought. Use estimation to help you decide who has enough money to pay for the purchases. Circle the names of the people who have enough money.

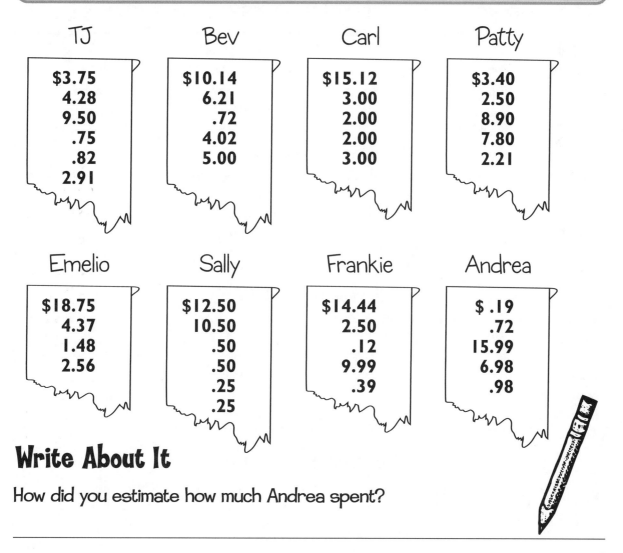

TJ	Bev	Carl	Patty
$3.75	$10.14	$15.12	$3.40
4.28	6.21	3.00	2.50
9.50	.72	2.00	8.90
.75	4.02	2.00	7.80
.82	5.00	3.00	2.21
2.91			

Emelio	Sally	Frankie	Andrea
$18.75	$12.50	$14.44	$ .19
4.37	10.50	2.50	.72
1.48	.50	.12	15.99
2.56	.50	9.99	6.98
	.25	.39	.98
	.25		

Write About It

How did you estimate how much Andrea spent?

_____

MONEY MATH

Counting Coins

Directions: For three months, the Zuk family saved coins in a jar. Each month, a family member saved only one kind of coin. Each month, each family member selected a different coin to save. Below is a chart of what each person saved for each of the three months. What is the total amount each person saved each month? We started the first month for you.

September Savings

FAMILY MEMBER	NUMBER OF COINS SAVED	TYPE OF COIN SAVED	TOTAL AMOUNT SAVED
Mr. Zuk	16	Half dollar (50¢)	$8.00
Mrs. Zuk	13	Quarter (25¢)	$3.25
Frannie	39	Dime (10¢)	_____
Stella Ann	11	Nickel (5¢)	_____
Tyrone	160	Penny (1¢)	_____

October Savings

FAMILY MEMBER	NUMBER OF COINS SAVED	TYPE OF COIN SAVED	TOTAL AMOUNT SAVED
Mr. Zuk	30	Quarter	_____
Mrs. Zuk	10	Nickel	_____
Frannie	98	Penny	_____
Stella Ann	8	Half dollar	_____
Tyrone	10	Dime	_____

November Savings

FAMILY MEMBER	NUMBER OF COINS SAVED	TYPE OF COIN SAVED	TOTAL AMOUNT SAVED
Mr. Zuk	25	Nickel	_____
Mrs. Zuk	316	Penny	_____
Frannie	10	Half dollar	_____
Stella Ann	20	Dime	_____
Tyrone	12	Quarter	_____

Write About It

Explain how you figured out how much 13 quarters are worth.

Unmasking Numbers

A bunch of numbers went to a masquerade ball. The host, Count Numero Uno, decided to have a contest and award a prize to any guest who could name every other guest. Each number was required to provide a clue about his or her identity. See how many numbered guests you can name using the clues provided.

MASKED GUEST #1:

4 more than me would give you 10. Who am I?

———————

MASKED GUEST #2:

One half of me is 8. Who am I?

———————

MASKED GUEST #3:

I am 12 more than 15. Who am I?

———————

MASKED GUEST #4:

20 years ago, I was 8 years old. Who am I?

———————

MASKED GUEST #5:

I am one half of 24. Who am I?

———————

MASKED GUEST #6:

You can name me if you multiply 6 and 8, then add 2 more to that number. Who am I?

———————

MASKED GUEST #7:

I am 30 minus 12. Who am I?

———————

MASKED GUEST #8:

If you know 7 x 7, then you know me. Who am I?

———————

MASKED GUEST #9:

I am 15 less than 36. Who am I?

———————

MASKED GUEST #10:

Double me and I'm 30. Who am I?

———————

PROBLEM SOLVING

Mental Math: Lightning Round!

Directions: Answer each question below as quickly as you can.

1. How many dimes equal a dollar?

   _____

2. How many legs do 7 hippopotamuses have?

   _____

3. How many quarters equal $5?

   _____

4. How many fingers do 12 people have?

   _____

5. How many paws do 10 dogs have?

   _____

6. How many tires do 300 cars have? (Include the spare tire in the trunk.)

   _____

7. How many eggs are in 4 dozen eggs?

   _____

8. How many nickels equal $2?

   _____

9. How many ounces are in 2 pounds? (16 ounces equal 1 pound)

   _____

10. How tall is Richard if Bob is 6 feet tall and Richard is half his size?

    _____

11. How many eyes do 9 bees have if each bee has 5 eyes?

    _____

12. How many teeth do two average people have if the average person has 32 teeth?

    _____

13. How many pages did I read if I started at the beginning of page 41 and stopped at the end of page 91?

    _____

14. How much will Leon spend on 3 bunches of flowers that cost $2.95 a bunch?

    _____

15. How many faces are there on 7 dice if each die has 6 faces?

    _____

Write About It

How did you use mental math to solve problem 14?

_____

_____

PROBLEM SOLVING

Number Search

Directions: Look at the group of numbers below. For each problem, search through the numbers and list those that solve the problem. There can be more than one answer for each problem.

10	7	18	5	1	6
8	3	19	2	9	12

1. Which numbers have a sum of 15?

   _____

2. Which numbers have a difference of 7?

   _____

3. Which numbers have a product of 21?

   _____

4. Which numbers have a sum that is 2 less than 12?

   _____

5. Which numbers have a product of 70?

   _____

6. Which numbers have a sum of 8 and a product of 15?

   _____

7. Which numbers have a sum that is equal to 3 x 9?

   _____

8. Which three numbers have a sum of 13?

   _____

9. Which numbers have a sum that is an odd number ending in 1?

   _____

10. Which three numbers have a product of 21?

    _____

11. If you divide one number by another number, the answer is 6. What are the two numbers?

    _____

12. If you divide these two numbers and multiply the quotient by 2, you get 8. What are the two numbers?

    _____

PROBLEM SOLVING

Batter Up!

Directions: Solve the baseball problems below.

1. There are 5 baseball players. The numbers on their uniforms are 1, 2, 3, 4, and 5. Arrange them in the field so that if you add their uniform numbers going across or up and down, the sum is 8. There are four ways to arrange the numbers.

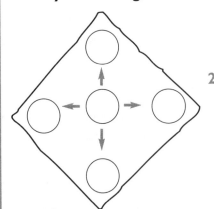

2. Arrange the same players so that when you add their uniform numbers across or up and down, the sum is 10.

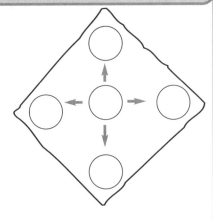

3. Arrange the same players so that when you add their uniform numbers across or up and down, the sum is 9.

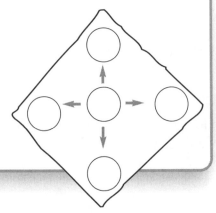

Name _____

Time, Please?

Look at the clock here.
What time does it say?

_____

Directions: Write the answer in the space provided.

1. **If it is 8:00 now, what time will it be in**
   a. 10 minutes? _____
   b. 15 minutes? _____
   c. 55 minutes? _____
   d. 1 hour and 10 minutes? _____
   e. 2 hours and 10 minutes? _____
   f. 1 hour and 2 minutes? _____
   g. 2 hours and 45 minutes? _____
   h. 2 hours and 36 minutes? _____
   i. 2 and 1/2 hours? _____
   j. 3 hours? _____

2. **If it is 8:00 now, what time was it**
   a. 10 minutes ago? _____
   b. 15 minutes ago? _____
   c. 13 minutes ago? _____
   d. 1 hour and 30 minutes ago? _____
   e. 25 minutes ago? _____
   f. 30 minutes ago? _____

g. 45 minutes ago? _____
h. 1 hour and 5 minutes ago? _____
i. 1 hour and 45 minutes ago? _____
j. 3 hours ago? _____

3. **If it is 8:06 now, what time will it be in**
   a. 5 minutes? _____
   b. 10 minutes? _____
   c. 25 minutes? _____
   d. 30 minutes? _____
   e. 33 minutes? _____

4. **If it is 8:06 now, what time was it**
   a. 5 minutes ago? _____
   b. 10 minutes ago? _____
   c. 25 minutes ago? _____
   d. 30 minutes ago? _____
   e. 33 minutes ago? _____

Write About It

Explain how you subtracted 30 minutes from 8:06 to get the answer.

_____

PROBLEM SOLVING

What Page Is Zeena on?

Directions: Answer each question below. Write your answer in the blanks.

1. **Zeena is reading an exciting story about spaceships. She is on page 46 of the story. What page would Zeena be on if she read**

   a.   3 more pages?   _____

   b.   10 more pages?   _____

   c.   20 more pages?   _____

   d.   40 more pages?   _____

   e.   50 more pages?   _____

2. **What page was Zeena on for each day of the week?**

   a.   On Friday, she was 10 pages back from page 46. She was on page _____.

   b.   On Thursday, she was 20 pages back from page 46. She was on page _____.

   c.   On Wednesday, she was 25 pages back from page 46. She was on page _____.

   d.   On Tuesday, she was 28 pages back from page 46. She was on page _____.

   e.   On Monday, she was 36 pages back from page 46. She was on page _____.

3. **Justin is reading a book about caring for a pet dog. He is on page 95.**

   a.   If he reads 15 more pages, he will be on page _____.

   b.   If he reads 10 more pages, he will be on page _____.

   c.   If he reads 23 more pages, he will be on page _____.

   d.   If he reads 39 more pages, he will be on page _____.

   e.   If he reads 50 more pages, he will be on page _____.

   f.   When he was 5 pages back from page 95, he was on page _____.

   g.   When he was 10 pages back from page 95, he was on page _____.

   h.   When he was 25 pages back from page 95, he was on page _____.

   i.   When he was 50 pages back from page 95, he was on page _____.

   j.   When he was 65 pages back from page 95, he was on page _____.

Write About It

Explain how you figure out what page Justin was on 50 pages ago, if he is on page 95 now.

PROBLEM SOLVING

Once Upon a Math

Once Upon a Math

Directions: Solve each problem using mental math. Write the answer in the blank after each problem.

1. Little Red Riding Hood bought 5 bouquets for her grandmother, Mrs. Wolf. Each bouquet cost $3. How much did she spend on the bouquets for Granny Wolf? _____

2. A Fredmobile holds 4 students going on a field trip to the dinosaur museum. How many Fredmobiles will Fred Flintstone need to transport Pebble's class of 28 students to the museum? _____

3. Snow White won $35 playing Bingo. She wants to give an equal amount of her winnings to each of the 7 dwarfs. How much does each dwarf receive?

   _____

4. Each page of Cinderella's photo album can hold 8 pictures. How many photos can she put in her album if the album has 9 pages? _____

5. Miss Piggy decided to buy Kermit a scarf and Elmo a hat for their birthdays. The scarf cost $6 and the hat cost $5. She gave the store clerk $15. How much change did she get back?

   _____

6. Pinocchio is having a pizza party. If one pizza feeds 6 people, how many pizzas are needed to feed 54 people?

   _____

7. Goldilocks is saving money for a new red cape that costs $27. She has saved $15 so far. How much more money does she need to save to buy her new red cape? _____

8. Sleeping Beauty needs her beauty sleep. She sleeps an average of 9 hours a day. At that rate, how many hours of beauty sleep does she get in one week? _____

9. Hansel and Gretel walk at the rate of 3 miles per hour. If they walked for 7 hours in the forest, did they walk more or less than 20 miles? _____

10. Humpty Dumpty measured his waist and found that it was 350 centimeters around. Old King Cole, the merry old soul, did the same. He measured 310 centimeters around. How many centimeters smaller around the waist is Old King Cole than Humpty Dumpty?

    _____

PROBLEM SOLVING

Math Tales

Directions: Figure out the year when the fairy-tale character did or will do his or her deed. Remember to use mental math.

1. It's the year 2000. The Three Little Pigs will wear wigs in 25 years. In what year will the pigs wear wigs?

   _____

2. It's the year 2000. The Goose That Laid the Golden Egg got a peg leg 10 years ago. In what year did the goose get the peg leg? _____

3. It's the year 2000. Tom Thumb will eat some plums 50 years from now. When will Tom Thumb start to eat plums? _____

4. It's the year 2000. Jack Frost got lost 25 years ago. In what year did Jack get lost? _____

5. It's the year 2000. Mary's Little Lamb never ate ham until 50 years ago. In what year did the lamb start to eat ham? _____

6. It's the year 2000. Little Bo Peep lost her sheep named Beep 35 years ago. In what year was Beep the sheep lost?

   _____

7. It's the year 2000. Cinderella will meet her fella, Jella, 125 years from now. In what year will Cinderella and her fella, Jella, meet? _____

8. It's the year 2000. In 201 years, Mother Hubbard, who will go to the cupboard to get her dog a bone, will find a stone instead. In what year will Mother Hubbard find a stone instead of a bone? _____

9. It's the year 2000. Babe the Blue Ox chased a fox from a box 90 years ago. When was the fox chased from the box by the ox? _____

10. It's the year 2000. Peter Piper will pick a peck of pickled peppers 40 years from now. When will that peck of pickled peppers be picked? _____

Write About It

How would you use mental math to find out how old 25-year-old Peter Piper was 13 years ago?

Name _____

Be a Number Detective

Directions: Read each clue carefully and figure out the secret number for each set of clues.

1. The number is less than 160.
   The number is greater than 145 + 5.
   The last digit is between 0 and 3.
   The number is odd.

   What is the number? _____

2. The number is more than 3 x 25.
   The number is less than 8 x 10.
   The sum of the digits is 14.
   The number is odd.

   What is the number? _____

3. The number is more than 2 x 17.
   The number is less than 2 x 19.
   The number is even.
   The number ends in a figure greater than 4.
   The number can be divided by 9.

   What is the number? _____

4. The number is greater than 3 x 100.
   The number is less than 400 – 50.
   The number is odd.
   The number does not end in 1, 3, 7, 9.
   The second digit is an even number less than 4, but more than 1.

   What is the number? _____

5. The number has two digits.
   The number's digits are the same.
   The number is odd.
   The sum of the digits in the number is less than 20, but greater than 17.

   What is the number? _____

6. The number is more than 4 x 6 x 25.
   The number ends in two zeros.
   The number is less than 800.
   The first digit is odd.

   What is the number? _____

7. The number is more than 7 x 9.
   The number is less than 8 x 9.
   The ones-place digit is greater than 6.
   The number is even.

   What is the number? _____

8. The number is less than 1,000.
   The number's digits are triplets.
   The digits are greater than 6.
   The number is even.

   What is the number? _____

NUMBER TRICKS

Subtraction Magic

Check out this subtraction magic. Amaze your friends by instantly subtracting a number from 1,000,000! Here's an example of how it's done:

Example:

Think: 2 + ? = 9   **1,000,000**   Think: 7 + ? = 10
             – 246,087

             753,913

Step 1: Start on the left. You get the first digit in your answer by thinking 2 + ? = 9. The answer is 7.

Step 2: For the next digit, think 4 + ? = 9. The answer is 5.

Step 3: For the next digit, think 6 + ? = 9. The answer is 3.

Step 4: For the next digit, think 0 + ? = 9. The answer is 9.

Step 5: For the next digit, think 8 + ? = 9. The answer is 1.

Step 6: For the last digit, think 7 + ? = 10. The answer is 3.

Directions: Try solving these problems using the trick above.

1.	10,000 – 4,862	3.	100 – 12	5.	1,000,000,000 – 427,678,914
2.	1,000 – 348	4.	100,000 – 36,987	6.	10,000 – 7,461

NUMBER TRICKS

Magic Mind-Reading Cards

Here's an easy trick for you to do for your friends.

Step 1: Give a friend a copy of the magic cards below.

Step 2: Ask your friend to pick a number from 1 to 31, but not to tell you.

Step 3: Tell your friend to point to all of the cards that have his or her number.

Step 4: Wave your hands over the magic cards and, in a mysterious voice, chant these words:

"Oh magic cards! Oh magic cards! Tell me which number my friend is thinking. Give me an inkling. Lucky 7, rabbit's foot, the owl says give me a hoot! Hocus Pocus let me find what's in my friend's mind, if you would be so kind."

How will you know what number your friend has picked? It's easy! Just add up the first numbers in each card that your friend pointed to. The sum of those first numbers is the number that your friend chose!

Here's an example: Say your friend, Joe, chose the number 9. He will point to the cards that have the number 9 in them. One of those cards starts with the number 1 and the other card starts with the number 8. You add $1 + 8$ and get the answer 9! After you make your chant, tell Joe that he picked the number 9.

Now, try the trick on your friends and family. Remember: To do the trick successfully, you should practice adding the first numbers on each card.

Magic Mind-Reading Cards

1	3	5	7
9	11	13	15
17	19	21	23
25	27	29	31

2	3	6	7
10	11	14	15
18	19	22	23
26	27	30	31

4	5	6	7
12	13	14	15
20	21	22	23
28	29	30	31

8	9	10	11
12	13	14	15
24	25	26	27
28	29	30	31

16	17	18	19
20	21	22	23
24	25	26	27
28	29	30	31

Magic Number Cards

Here's an easy number trick you can do for your friends.

Step 1: Cut out the cards below and give them to a friend.

Step 2: Ask your friend to pick a card and tell you the number above the box. Tell him or her that you will then reveal the number that is in the box.

Here's how the trick is done:

Add 8 to the number your friend gives you. Then reverse the digits of the answer you get. If you get a 0 in an answer after you add 8, keep the 0 when you reverse the digits. For example, 20 becomes 02. Next, add the two digits to get the third and last digit of the number in the box.

Example: Your friend picks card #10. Add 8 + 10 to get 18. Then reverse the digits so 18 becomes 81. 8 and 1 are the first two digits of the number in the box. Finally, add 8 + 1 to get the last digit of the number: 9. So, the number in the box that your friend picked is 819.

#19	#8	#3	#9
729	617	112	718

#23	#1	#15	#17
134	909	325	527

#7	#21	#10	#22
516	921	819	033

#18	#2	#4	#24
628	011	213	235

NUMBER TRICKS

Math Marvel

Here's a fun addition trick you can do for your friends. You will be able to give the answer to a problem before the numbers in the problem are added together! Here's how:

Step 1: You'll need at least four people to do this trick.

Step 2: Ask Person A to write a three-digit number on a piece of paper. Make sure everyone can see the number he or she wrote. Say, Person A wrote the number 847.

Step 3: On another piece of paper, you write 2,845. Fold it and give it to Person B to hold. Tell Person B not to look at the number. No one should look at the number until you complete the trick. Why do you write 2,845?

To do the trick, you need to put the number 2 in front of the first digit of Person A's number. Then repeat the first two numbers of Person A's number (8 and 4). Finally, subtract 2 from the last digit of Person A's number (7 – 2) and write the difference (5) as the last digit of your number.

Step 4: Ask Person C to write a three-digit number on the same piece of paper that Person A wrote his or her number. Make sure that Person C's number is below Person A's number. Say Person C wrote 258. So the piece of paper would look like this:

847
258

Step 5: Write 741 underneath 258. Why? You need to subtract each of the digits in Person C's number from 9. So you subtract 9 – 2 to get 7, 9 – 5 to get 4, and 9 – 8 to get 1. Your number is 741.

Step 6: Ask Person D to write a three-digit number below your number. Say Person D writes 307.

Step 7: Using the same strategy you used in Step 5, you write 692 underneath 307. To get 692, you subtract 9 – 3, 9 – 0, and 9 – 7.

Step 8: Ask all the people participating to add all the numbers on the first piece of paper together:

847	(Person A's number)
258	(Person C's number)
741	(Your first number)
307	(Person D's number)
+ 692	(Your second number)
2,845	(Sum)

Step 9: Ask Person B to unfold the piece of paper you gave him or her and read the number on it. Your audience will be amazed that it's the same number as the sum of all the other numbers.

Step 10: Take a bow and enjoy the applause.

Answers

Look for Easy Numbers for E-Z Addition (page 9)
1. 15
2. 19
3. 14
4. 18
5. 17
6. 27
7. 40
8. 26
9. 38
10. 47
11. 68
12. 83

Look for More Easy Numbers in Addition (page 10)
1. 22
2. 27
3. 43
4. 45
5. 80
6. 97
7. 62
8. 114
9. 140
10. 190
11. 60
12. 93
13. 140
14. 362
15. 442

Make Easy Numbers Using 10 and 100 (page 11)
1. f
2. a
3. k
4. h
5. e
6. b
7. j
8. c
9. i
10. g
11. l
12. d

Using Patterns of 10 (page 12)
1. 62
2. 67
3. 33
4. 61
5. 80
6. 62
7. 82
8. 161
9. 103
10. 437
11. 539
12. 654
13. 862
14. 735
15. 1,475
16. 3,274
17. 5,505
18. 7,852

Breaking Up Numbers Is Easy to Do! (page 13)
1. 78
2. 99
3. 98
4. 38
5. 59
6. 99
7. 109
8. 89
9. 95
10. 99
11. 35
12. 33
13. 13
14. 31
15. 35
16. 23
17. 16
18. 21
19. 25
20. 25

Breaking Up for Multiplication and Division (page 14)
1. 36
2. 155
3. 248
4. 86
5. 96
6. 54
7. 180
8. 104
9. 168
10. 216
11. 6
12. 7
13. 6
14. 8
15. 13
16. 12
17. 15
18. 12
19. 16
20. 12

10 Is a Friend! (page 15)
1. 17
2. 11
3. 14
4. 13
5. 13
6. 12
7. 15
8. 12
9. 11
10. 14

9 Is Fine! (page 16)
1. 15
2. 11
3. 13
4. 16
5. 18
6. 14
7. 12
8. 17
9. 11
10. 13

Strategies for Adding 9 to a Number (page 17)
1. 23
2. 37
3. 46
4. 54
5. 75
6. 92
7. 106
8. 215
9. 426
10. 534
11. 883
12. 991
13. 1,872
14. 2,453
15. 6,295
16. 7,656
17. 5,244
18. 5,523
19. 4,467
20. 1,312

Easy Numbers Make Happy Faces! (page 19)
1. 45 + 20 = 65
2. 20 + 64 = 84
3. 20 + 47 = 67
4. 73 + 20 = 93
5. 69 + 10 = 79
6. 15 + 80 = 95

Patterns in the One–Hundred Chart (page 22)
1. Yes; yes; The pattern continues.
2. 1
3. 2; yes
4. Yes; Even-number columns are those that start with 2, 4, 6, 8, and 10, while the odd-number columns start with 1, 3, 5, 7, and 9.
5. If you count by twos starting with 2, the numbers you count are even. If you start with 3 and count by twos, the numbers you count are odd.
6. Answers will vary.
7. Each number is 10 more than the number above it. Answers will vary.
8. 14; Answers will vary.
9. 17; Answers will vary.
10. A diagonal

Follow the Pattern (page 23)
1. 2, 12, 22, 32, 42, 52, 62, 72, 82, 92
2. 10, 20, 30, 40, 50, 60, 70, 80, 90, 100
3. 5, 15, 25, 35, 45, 55, 65, 75, 85, 95
4. 8, 18, 28, 38, 48, 58, 68, 78, 88, 98
5. 4, 14, 24, 34, 44, 54, 64, 74, 84, 94

No Looking! What's Missing? (page 24)

After and Before Numbers (page 25)
1. 21
2. 46
3. 55
4. 38
5. 72
6. 77
7. 95
8. 86
9. 104
10. 109
11. 53
12. 30
13. 94
14. 70
15. 105
16. 75
17. 92
18. 60
19. 102
20. 110
21. 2
22. 6
23. 7
24. 5
25. 20
26. 16
27. 30
28. 25
29. 42
30. 50
31. 71
32. 46
33. 60
34. 67
35. 84
36. 60
37. 63
38. 72
39. 89
40. 88

Skip to My 2s (page 26)
1. 12, 14, 16
2. 26, 28, 30, 32, 34
3. 48, 50, 52, 54, 56
4. 80, 82, 84, 86, 88
5. 104, 106, 108, 110, 112
6. 9, 11, 13, 15, 17
7. 27, 29, 31, 33, 35
8. 59, 61, 63, 65, 67
9. 85, 87, 89, 91, 93
10. 103, 105, 107, 109, 111

Skip to My 2s ... Backwards! (page 27)
1. 6, 4, 2
2. 34, 32, 30, 28, 26
3. 82, 80, 78, 76, 74
4. 94, 92, 90, 88, 86
5. 102, 100, 98, 96, 94
6. 144, 142, 140, 138, 136
7. 11, 9, 7, 5, 3
8. 15, 13, 11, 9, 7
9. 31, 29, 27, 25, 23
10. 59, 57, 55, 53, 51

Ladders and Chutes (page 28)
Ladders:

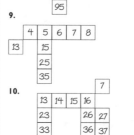

Chutes:

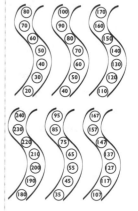

Follow the Winding Brick Road! (page 29)

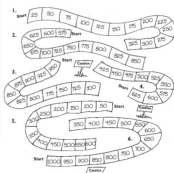

78

Lucky 7 (page 30)

1. 7
2. 17
3. 27
4. 37
5. 47
6. 57
7. 67
8. 70
9. 71
10. 72

11. 73
12. 74
13. 75
14. 76
15. 77
16. 78
17. 79
18. 87
19. 97

There are twenty 7s in all.

Doubles are No Trouble! (page 32)

1. 10
2. 4
3. 14
4. 6
5. 2
6. 8
7. 16
8. 12
9. 18

10. 4 + 4
11. 2 + 2
12. 9 + 9
13. 5 + 5
14. 8 + 8
15. 3 + 3
16. 1 + 1
17. 7 + 7
18. 6 + 6

Double the Number, Double the Fun! (page 33)

2. 9, 18, 36
3. 7, 14, 28
4. 8, 16, 32
5. 1, 2, 4
6. 10, 20, 40
7. 5, 10, 20
8. 6, 12, 24
9. 3, 6, 12
10. 4, 8, 16

E-Z Strategy Using Doubles (page 34)

1. 16, 17, 15
2. 14, 13, 15
3. 10, 11, 9
4. 18, 17, 19
5. 12, 11, 13
6. 20, 21, 19

You Can Half It! (page 35)

1. 2
2. 3
3. 5
4. 10
5. 30
6. 40
7. 50
8. 200
9. 300
10. 400

How Many Beans Are in the Pot? (page 36)

1. 5
2. 5
3. 5
4. 5
5. 7
6. 9
7. 8
8. 7
9. 3
10. 7

What's the Missing Number? (page 37)

1. 5
2. 2
3. 3
4. 4
5. 2
6. 8
7. 4
8. 3
9. 7
10. 9

11. 7
12. 8
13. 8
14. 7
15. 9
16. 5
17. 9
18. 9
19. 6
20. 9

It's All in the Number Family! (page 38)

1. $5 + 4 = 9$
   $4 + 5 = 9$
   $9 - 5 = 4$
   $9 - 4 = 5$
2. $3 + 8 = 11$
   $8 + 3 = 11$
   $11 - 3 = 8$
   $11 - 8 = 3$
3. $4 + 6 = 10$
   $6 + 4 = 10$
   $10 - 4 = 6$
   $10 - 6 = 4$
4. $7 + 6 = 13$
   $6 + 7 = 13$
   $13 - 7 = 6$
   $13 - 6 = 7$
5. $8 + 4 = 12$
   $4 + 8 = 12$
   $12 - 8 = 4$
   $12 - 4 = 8$
6. $6 + 5 = 11$
   $5 + 6 = 11$
   $11 - 6 = 5$
   $11 - 5 = 6$
7. $9 + 7 = 16$
   $7 + 9 = 16$
   $16 - 9 = 7$
   $16 - 7 = 9$
8. $9 + 6 = 15$
   $6 + 9 = 15$
   $15 - 9 = 6$
   $15 - 6 = 9$
9. $7 + 6 = 13$
   $6 + 7 = 13$
   $13 - 7 = 6$
   $13 - 6 = 7$
10. $7 + 8 = 15$
    $8 + 7 = 15$
    $15 - 7 = 8$
    $15 - 8 = 7$
11. $8 + 5 = 13$
    $5 + 8 = 13$
    $13 - 8 = 5$
    $13 - 5 = 8$
12. $4 + 7 = 11$
    $7 + 4 = 11$
    $11 - 4 = 7$
    $11 - 7 = 4$

+/– Flash Cards (page 39)

1. 3
2. 5
3. 9
4. 7
5. 4
6. 8
7. 4
8. 8
9. 9
10. 6

x/÷ Flash Cards (page 40)

1. 7
2. 4
3. 7
4. 7
5. 9
6. 7
7. 6
8. 7
9. 6
10. 4

Don't Carry That 10! (page 41)

1. 4̲1̲ 38; 9̲1̲ 88; 58 6̲1̲; 19 2̲2̲; 29 3̲2̲
2. 1̲1̲ 4; 5̲1̲ 44; 8̲2̲ 75; 36 4̲3̲; 89 9̲6̲
3. 2̲5̲ 17; 8̲1̲ 73; 7̲6̲ 68; 76 8̲4̲; 35 4̲3̲
4. 3̲6̲ 27; 9̲4̲ 85; 41 5̲0̲; 18 2̲7̲; 68 7̲7̲
5. 3̲4̲ 29; 8̲2̲ 77; 4̲1̲ 36; 87 9̲2̲; 19 2̲4̲
6. 9̲3̲ 87; 5̲1̲ 45; 79 8̲5̲; 68 7̲4̲; 36 4̲2̲

Adding 100s and 1,000s (page 42)

1. 132
2. 142
3. 167
4. 200
5. 207
6. 413
7. 701
8. 828
9. 999
10. 624
11. 1,000
12. 2,714
13. 1,505
14. 8,988
15. 5,521
16. 5,115

17. 5,000
18. 3,127
19. 1,211
20. 6,590
21. 1,037
22. 1,195
23. 1,440
24. 1,099
25. 1,457
26. 1,053
27. 6,516
28. 7,041
29. 8,507
30. 5,007
31. 3,234
32. 5,773

Hit the Target Number! (page 43)

1. $100 + 200$
   $200 + 100$
   $250 + 50$
   $150 + 150$
   $50 + 250$
   $125 + 175$
2. $300 + 200$
   $100 + 400$
   $450 + 50$
   $350 + 150$
   $475 + 25$
   $425 + 75$
3. $100 + 900$
   $800 + 200$
   $600 + 400$
   $550 + 450$
   $300 + 700$
   $50 + 950$
4. $800 + 50$
   $825 + 25$
   $750 + 100$
   $725 + 125$
   $700 + 150$
   $600 + 250$
5. $600 + 92$
   $690 + 2$
   $680 + 12$
   $650 + 42$
   $675 + 17$
   $686 + 6$

Subtracting From 100 Is Easy – Part 2 (page 45)

1. 57
2. 49
3. 13
4. 32
5. 65
6. 78
7. 83
8. 61
9. 29
10. 42
11. 74
12. 23

Pick a Pair of Pears (page 46)

1. 10
2. 30
3. 70
4. 10
5. 50
6. 30
7. 50
8. $50 + 30$ or $70 + 10$
9. $50 + 10$ or $30 + 30$
10. $10 + 90$ or $70 + 30$ or $50 + 50$
11. $70 + 30$ or $10 + 90$ or $50 + 50$
12. $90 + 30$ or $70 + 50$
13. $70 + 50$ or $90 + 30$
14. $90 + 70$

Number Chain Links (page 47)

1. 9
2. 2
3. 6
4. 25
5. 20
6. 22
7. 20
8. 600

Mental Math Can Save Time (page 49)

1. 99
2. 100
3. 94
4. 100
5. 301
6. 700
7. 10
8. 144
9. 800
10. 405
11. 40
12. 150
13. 80
14. 50
15. 100
16. 800

Letter Have Values, Too! (page 50)

1. 45
2. 30
3. 150
4. 145
5. 160
6. 70
7. 145
8. 135
9. 185
10. 220

11. 85
12. 225
13. 85
14. 130
15. 110
16. 235
17. 30
18. 225
19. 85
20. 45

Calculate on Your Calculator (page 51)

1. + 1
2. + 20
3. + 100
4. – 20
5. – 2,000

6. + 3,000
7. + 6
8. + 60
9. – 76
10. – 300

Exercise Your Number Sense (page 52)

	+ 1,000	+ 99	+ 100	– 11	+ 11	– 9	+ 9	– 5	+ 5	– 10	+ 10	
	1,024	123	124	13	35	15	33	19	29	14	34	24
	1,082	181	182	71	93	73	91	77	87	72	92	82
	1,051	150	151	40	62	42	60	46	56	41	61	51
	1,017	116	117	6	28	8	26	12	22	7	27	17
	1,090	189	190	94	101	81	99	85	95	80	100	90
	1,105	204	205	119	116	96	114	100	110	95	115	105
	1,130	229	230	154	141	121	139	125	135	120	140	130
	1,165	264	265	381	176	156	174	160	170	155	175	165
	1,392	491	492	488	403	383	401	387	397	382	402	392
	1,499	598	599		510	490	508	494	504	489	509	499

Circle the Largest Answer (page 53)

1. 35 + 2
2. 13 – 5
3. 145 + 0
4. 19 + 5
5. 25 + 10
6. 100 – 10
7. 20 + 40
8. 100 + 40
9. 11 + 90
10. 1,000 + 50

The Largest Number in a Diamond (page 54)
1. 350 – 2
2. 25
3. 5 x 25
4. 301 x 4
5. 500 + 400
6. 6 x 7
7. 50 + 25
8. 60 – 8
9. 600 – 150
10. 20 + 20
11. 13,000 – 200
12. $3.95 + $3.95

In Your Estimation . . . (page 55)
1. a, b, c, d
2. a, e
3. a. 4   b. 4   c. 3
   d. 3   e. 4   f. 3
4. a. underestimate
   b. underestimated
   c. overestimate
   d. underestimate

Shape Up With Numbers! (page 56)
1. square = 8; triangle = 3
2. square = 7; circle = 4
3. circle = 9
4. circle = 8; triangle = 7
5. triangle = 5; square = 3
6. square = 7
7. circle = 9; square = 6
8. triangle = 8; square = 4
9. circle = 8; square = 6

Concentration: Mental-Math Style (page 57)
A matches K
C matches M
F matches D
H matches P
I matches E
L matches J
N matches G
O matches B

What's Left? (page 58)
1. 1   16. 2
2. 0   17. 1
3. 1   18. 4
4. 2   19. 0
5. 0   20. 0
6. 1   21. 4
7. 2   22. 0
8. 0   23. 2
9. 2   24. 1
10. 3   25. 2
11. 2   26. 3
12. 1   27. 0
13. 1   28. 4
14. 0   29. 0
15. 1   30. 1

What's Your Change? (page 59)
1. 90 cents   10. 50 cents
2. 20 cents   11. 75 cents
3. 25 cents   12. 80 cents
4. 2 cents   13. 1 cent
5. 10 cents   14. 6 cents
6. 92 cents   15. 9 cents
7. 15 cents   16. 40 cents
8. 70 cents   17. 39 cents
9. 85 cents   18. 60 cents

How Much Is in the Piggy Bank? (page 60)
Karen $2.27
Thomas $.75
Alvin $1.01
Rosita $7.38
Ricky $17.30
Marta $3.52

Calculator-Free Shopping (pages 61–62)
Ken $4.25
Olivia $8.00
Annette $6.25
Bella $5.75
Todd $3.50
Marianne $6.50
Ben $6.50
Brian $18.00
Tucker $4.00

Who Has Enough Money? (page 63)
TJ, Patty, Sally, and Andrea

Counting Coins (page 64)
September
Frannie saved $3.90
Stella Ann saved $.55
Tyrone saved $1.60
October
Mr Zuk saved $7.50
Mrs. Zuk saved $.50
Frannie saved $.98
Stella Ann saved $4.00
Tyrone saved $1.00
November
Mr. Zuk saved $1.25
Mrs. Zuk saved $3.16
Frannie saved $5.00
Stella Ann saved $2.00
Tyrone saved $3.00

Unmasking Numbers (page 65)
Masked Guest #1: 6
Masked Guest #2: 16
Masked Guest #3: 27
Masked Guest #4: 28
Masked Guest #5: 12
Masked Guest #6: 50
Masked Guest #7: 18
Masked Guest #8: 49
Masked Guest #9: 21
Masked Guest #10: 15

Mental Math: Lightning Round (page 66)
1. 10 dimes
2. 28 legs
3. 20 quarters
4. 120 fingers
5. 40 paws
6. 1,500 tires
7. 48 eggs
8. 40 nickels
9. 32 ounces
10. 3 feet
11. 45 eyes
12. 64 teeth
13. 50 pages
14. $8.85
15. 42 faces

Number Search (page 67)
1. Answers will vary
2. Answers will vary
3. 7 x 3, 7 x 3 x 1
4. Answers will vary
5. 10 x 7
6. 3 and 5
7. 8 + 19 and 9 + 18
8. Answers will vary
9. Answers will vary
10. 1 x 3 x 7
11. 12 and 2 or 18 and 3
    or 6 and 1
12. 12 and 3 or 8 and 2

Batter Up! (page 68)

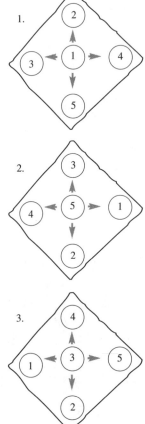

Time, Please? (page 69)
1. a. 8:10   3. a. 8:11
   b. 8:15   b. 8:16
   c. 8:55   c. 8:31
   d. 9:10   d. 8:36
   e. 10:10   e. 8:39
   f. 9:02
   g. 10:45
   h. 10:36
   i. 10:30
   j. 11:00

2. a. 7:50   4. a. 8:01
   b. 7:45   b. 7:56
   c. 7:47   c. 7:41
   d. 6:30   d. 7:36
   e. 7:35   e. 7:33
   f. 7:30
   g. 7:15
   h. 6:55
   i. 6:15
   j. 5:00

What Page Is Zeena On? (page 70)
1. a. page 49   3. a. page 110
   b. page 56   b. page 105
   c. page 66   c. page 118
   d. page 86   d. page 134
   e. page 96   e. page 145
2. a. page 36   f. page 90
   b. page 26   g. page 85
   c. page 21   h. page 70
   d. page 18   i. page 45
   e. page 10   j. page 30

Once Upon a Math (page 71)
1. $15
2. 7 Fredmobiles
3. $5
4. 72 photos
5. $4
6. 9 pizzas
7. $12
8. 63 hours
9. more
10. 40 centimeters

Math Tales (page 72)
1. 2025   6. 1965
2. 1990   7. 2125
3. 2050   8. 2201
4. 1975   9. 1910
5. 1950   10. 2040

Be a Number Detective (page 73)
1. 151   5. 99
2. 77   6. 700
3. 36   7. 68
4. 325   8. 888

Subtraction Magic (page 74)
1. 5,138
2. 652
3. 88
4. 63,013
5. 572,321,086
6. 2,539